PHOTO JOURNAL

Place
Pictures
Here

Place
Pictures
Here

Place
Pictures
Here

Place
Pictures
Here

Place
Pictures
Here

Place
Pictures
Here

Place
Pictures
Here

Place
Pictures
Here

Place
Pictures
Here

Place
Pictures
Here

Place
Pictures
Here

Place
Pictures
Here

Place
Pictures
Here

Place
Pictures
Here

Place
Pictures
Here

Place
Pictures
Here

Place
Pictures
Here

Place
Pictures
Here

Place
Pictures
Here

Place
Pictures
Here

Place
Pictures
Here

Place
Pictures
Here

Place
Pictures
Here

Place
Pictures
Here

Place
Pictures
Here

Place
Pictures
Here

Place
Pictures
Here

Place
Pictures
Here

Place
Pictures
Here

Place
Pictures
Here

Place
Pictures
Here

Place
Pictures
Here

Place
Pictures
Here

Place
Pictures
Here

Place
Pictures
Here

Place
Pictures
Here

Place
Pictures
Here

Place
Pictures
Here

Place
Pictures
Here

Place
Pictures
Here

Place
Pictures
Here

Place
Pictures
Here

Place
Pictures
Here

Place
Pictures
Here

Place
Pictures
Here

Place
Pictures
Here

Place
Pictures
Here

Place
Pictures
Here

www.ingramcontent.com/pod-product-compliance
Lightning Source LLC
LaVergne TN
LVHW082301150826
845677LV00009B/1686

* 9 7 9 8 8 6 9 4 5 5 3 6 9 *